OUTSIDE THE MARGIN OF ERROR

A Prison Poem Collection

Aaron M. Kinzer

Table of Contents

Acknowledgements:
A Letter from Aaron

I would like to thank my mother, Corliss Bradford, and brother, Anthony Kinzer, Jr., for their unwavering support before, during and after my incarceration. I am forever indebted to them.

I would also like to thank my kids, Jaidan, Jasiah, and Jeremiah for keeping me in their hearts and minds while I was absent from their lives. Thank you all for giving me a second chance at being a good dad. To my father, Anthony Kinzer, Sr., thank you for always believing in me.

I would be remiss not to acknowledge my good friend and podcast co-host Chris "Unctie C" Davis for his many hours of work on this project. He has been a force of encouragement from the first conversation we had at the halfway house. I, too, must thank the groups on the inside that gave me a microphone to speak.

Lastly, I owe a big thanks to my Augusta, GA poetry community and in particular 'God Brother Trav', Sa-Jules, Big Bailey, and Most Elevated Deepness for putting me on stages across the city. Photos of me after incarceration included in this collection are by *4Life Photography* in Augusta, Ga.

Peace,

Aaron "ONELOVE" Kinzer

ONE

Aaron M. Kinzer

Journalist. Poet. Motivational Speaker

FOREWARD

I first met Aaron at the halfway house in Augusta where he was finishing his bid receiving re-entry and transition services that were all but beneficial. The halfway house was plagued with jaded administration that seemingly thrived on perpetuating the oppression intrinsically rooted within the prison system.

As I got to know and be around Aaron, I noticed that he was always imparting wisdom to the guys in his dorm and everyone at the center who would lend an ear – it was apparent that this man had a message to share. I knew that this was a soul who had an experience that must be represented and a perspective that is needed to shed light into the darkness of mass incarceration and imprisonment [***legalized slavery***] in America.

To you, Aaron, I congratulate you on your accomplishments and I commend your strength, your endurance, and your unwavering dedication to making a difference and changing the narrative. I appreciate your motivation, your encouragement, and for believing in my vision for Safe Spaces & Faces Podcast. I'm thankful for your friendship and the wisdom that you've shared with me. Keep your head high, keep your focus sharp, and do the damn thing, bro.

To the readers: I implore you to read this collection from Aaron's perspective – allow yourself to be vulnerable to FEEL every moment, every feeling, every fleeting joy, every painful word that you read. Let Aaron transport you along his journey of grief, understanding, perseverance, aggravation, and triumph. Without further ado, here is *Outside the Margin of Error: A Prison Poem Collection*.

Christopher "Unctie C" Davis

To the millions of people incarcerated around the world, this is for you. I am your voice.

-Aaron

INNER PARTS

Cast into the belly of the beast.
Thrown down and out of sight.
The stench is upon me, and I might
Succumb to the weight as it is heavy on my head.
Rest I am seeking for body and soul but I'm without comfort in bed.
I lay on steel and concrete.
Walk without shoes on feet.
Longing for sunlight so I may bask in heat.

The screams of men pierce my silence.
Others fall prey to self-violence.

Some never leave, entering without escape.
A perpetual presence in this belly without a release date.

A call, a note, or hand reaching from beyond is our singular request.
A friendly expression of sympathy, empathy or even less
Is what we will accept
And do away with what we expect
From those who express a desire to connect... with our plight.
They don't know this fight. Eyes not seen this sight.

Yesterday my garments were worn by my neighbor.
So I can defecate, I ask you to turn your head as a favor.
Tangle that scent with the flavor
Of a meal served through a hole and beside a toilet bowl.
Don't flush this vision just yet.

My towel is washcloth that remains unfresh and wet
Because the air is thick with flatulence and sweat.

Outside the Margin of Error

The walls are moist and damp.
The night is lost by the light of a lamp
That fills every corner of my view.

Every day is old but begins anew.

The jangle of keys, bootsteps and count. I am only a number on the list.
And only in my slumber do I get to miss
The horrors that accompany such a scene as this
With a goodbye kiss I blow away the pleasantries of bliss
And adapt to my surroundings.
I'm in lockstep with the rhythm of my heart-pounding.
I thirst for more sound things.

I am without a familiar flavor to savor.

The harmonies of slammed doors and sweet melodies of radio static
Greet me as I return from my attic... of distant thoughts.
For a moment briefly I got away.
Immersed in my dream of the day
The trees in the breeze I saw sway
And a marvelous maiden lying in wait.
What I only anticipate
Is the smile of my son casting eyes on his father's face,
The joy of my wife as I lift her veil of lace,
Drying the tears of my daughter as they moisten her face.
I offer peaceful prayers thanking God for good grace.

Upon my release I'll only return to a larger enclosed space
Leaving many brethren behind.
Left to feast in the belly of the beast and create monstrous
Memories while doing time.

PUBLIC LYNCHING

THE STATE:

Your Honor, We the People, believe the defendant is a danger to
the public and in order to keep them safe
The People moves this court to remand the criminal to custody
for many years with haste,
Record a picture of their face
And mark the file in our database.

Your Honor, this miscreant has broken our laws and norms,
Shot shots with perfect form
And caused more damage to lives than perfect storms.

They have peddled poison and pistols,
Dashed hopes and crushed crystal... dreams.
Their schemes of homicide and robbery will probably
Never allow peace to return to ruined lives.
Drug addicted husbands and wives
Remain in the wake of their felonious wave.

The People, Your Honor, recommend a harsh punishment in order to
deter future criminals who wish to behave, in such a fashion.
Your Honor, the defendant terrorized our civil society with passion
And their actions... are without excuse.

DEFENDANT:

Your Honor, allow me the use
Of this moment with the courts attention
To make mention
Of my sincere regret that I am before you in this capacity
Shackled at my wrist and ankles while the law laughs at me.

The people splash my past at me,
Serve me on a platter for you to take a stab at me.
But those actions are now in the back of me

And fail to tell a two-sided story,
For my rise to glory
Was stunted at a too-young age.

Outside the Margin of Error

As a youngster the pimps and hustlers were all the rage
The money, guns, and drugs were more than a faze
As a matter of fact you would be amazed
If you witnessed the battle that was waged

For my tender young mind.

The efforts duplicated prior times
In which an unseen force assisted our crimes.

Powder and rocks seemingly fell from the sky;
I witnessed mothers sell their bodies to get high.
Dad left at an early age without saying goodbye.
You know this mix makes for a tasteless pie,

Now you wish to take a slice of my life.
Shame on you twice. The look in your eye is cold as ice,

Indifferent attitude toward the foes I face
Caring less if my life's a waste,
Recite the law and swing your gavel,
Sentence me to confinement, let my life unravel.
Correction or rehab, neither is your aim.
The 13th amendment spells out your game.

As I close
Let me remind you that that life is not the life I chose.
To be honest I have yet to choose,
As a growing young man still I have my forever to lose,
Keep that in mind, Your Honor, as you contemplate my fate.

I ask you to find a way to un-foster your hate
Before you decide on how long to lock me behind the gate.

Outside the Margin of Error

THE JUDGE:

Young man,
your eloquent allocution heaps heavy weight on this court.
And stories like yours will impact all decisions going forth.
However, I am forced

To consider the facts of your acts that brought you here today
How you endangered public safety as your personal field of play
So let me say...

That with the power vested in me by the law and The Lord Jesus Christ
I wash my hands of any regrets as I sentence you to life.

THIS CALL

My thirteen year old son pressed five to accept my call
Told me him and his friends were walking downtown after school
My mind saw Tamir at the park.
Jeremiah had just walked away from one
On the phone and on his way into the land of commerce
His value is decreasing with every step
In comparison to antique rugs and jewelry he's practically worthless
His being is secondary to java and subs and billiards on the border.

From my post on the phone I felt my son alone exposed and prone
To the guardians of commerce and wealth.
I saw Elijah walking from the store
In the shadows of a historic train station
A replica of ancestral depots.

I knew he walked, he and his boys
Him, extremely light-skinned but just black enough.

Through the phone his breathing was rapid
Motionless, mine was too.
My thoughts raced like the moment, what could his violations be?
What would some bad apple see? A threat to democracy?

A boy too tall for thirteen?
Some black-ass high-yella boy likely to commit felony
Because his Dad's in prison?
I twitched with fear. Made small talk.
"Do you have money?" Trying to insinuate that he has no reason to steal.
No reason to draw the attention of the commerce guards.
"Have you called your mom? Where is she at?"
I saw Michael Brown in a store

I stayed calm under assault from years-ago news loops
Bullet holes in teen boys, Black, state issued rifles
Protests, riots, prayers, and Bibles
Not for my son, my boy, my hope. I hope. "He son," I say, "do you have your bookbag?
Are you wearing a hoodie?" -- This is a call from a Federal Pri-...
"Hello..."

SAPPHIRE DICE

The tears of my lost soul
splash
Into lava-like lakes and
crash
As waves onto the shores of hot coals.
I've been burned.
Through my trials I've earned
the stripes.
The chinks in my armor
And missing links in my chain
Expose my pain.
What's my loss? My gain?

Internally I glow as embers on wildfire nights;
Formerly blue from gambling with sapphire dice.
Took chances at love, living huge wire life.
Boldly stepping, I fell through ice.
Reaching my hand I saw your silhouette shift in distance.
That was the instance,
Dawning on me at dawn, you were gone.

SOLDIERS OF JUSTICE

Dream Corps Justice
stands on the front lines for me.
Building bridges
across gaps of empathy.

Forming bonds with those of us
who languish inside.
Detached from habitats
where we used to reside.

Holding hands of those
reaching from the abyss:
America's prison institution,
none peculiar as this.

Raising voices
on the platform loud.
Making special
a nameless face in the crowd.

At the bottom of the well
your special wishes sink down to me.
Prayers and amazing grace
now helps me see.

Social justice warriors
unsheathe thy sword
As Dream Corps leads
and we march with one accord.

DOUBLE EDGED SWORD

My kids left behind without a dad
I was caught up in a paper chase like a fad.

Chasing my tail in a circle with no direction
Plugged into a life with no connection.

Late night drug raids, swat kicked in the door
Long guns with red lights, I knelt to the floor.

Kids sleep in the bed, violated their peace
America's war on drugs finally hit home for me
My ol' lady in jail, denied bail, blame it on me
I'm in jail on the phone talking recklessly.

All calls on tape, they were recording me
Used every word as evidence in my discovery.

Four years pre-trial, fought hard to no avail
Prosecutors' pressure made my family tell.

Facing 25 got 15, how should I feel?
There's a double-edged sword to keeping it real.

I walk any yard crew-thick or by myself
Paperwork on deck keeps me in good health.

Salutes from soldiers that share this struggle
But now my ol' lady got a new man to cuddle
I'm missing my sons' games and plays in the huddle.

My daughter shoots hoops and hits home runs
I tell her over the phone to do her best and have fun.

Outside the Margin of Error

My oldest going off to college and I got one that don't speak
How long have I been gone now? Who can count the weeks?

I could have told on you and traded places
Lit birthday candle and saw smiling faces
Took her to the dentist to get those braces
Cheer my baby on as she ran the bases.

But I kept it one-hundred and now I'm 10 yrs. in
I lost my family and can't get it back again
I'll hold back the tears and tuck them back within
Because I have a few more' nights left till my future begins.

ALLOCUTION

My legs tremble as I offer the court reasons
Not to lock me away for over one hundred seasons.

Shackled at the ankles, wrist and around my waist
Voice cracking and eyes blurry while looking the judge in face
Stuttering over my words, the ones I'm able to find
I can see justice peeking because she was never blind.

Your Honor, admit that I've led a life of crime
And six months in the city jail should have been a sign

That if I keep on things will only get worse
State prison or Fed., whichever gets me first.

I should have listened when my mom begged me to stop
But I had my eyes focused on the hustler's mountain top,

I was blinded by the speed of the night
Believing that in the drug game I could take flight.

Endless floods of dollars were too much for my mind
Even though I knew guys that got lots of time.

I remained unable to change
Told myself every day that I should get out of the game
But the thought of poverty brought searing pain.

So, I doubled down and bought more coke
Unaware of the destruction, dashing hopes
Ignoring the warning signs and slippery slopes
I laughed at the law as a joke.

Outside the Margin of Error

Too young to know better and too young to care
Assisted in atrocities now I expect you to be fair.

But what is fair is unknown to the masses
Can you be impartial despite our different classes?

Can you judge the crimes but also consider the cause?
Will you use discretion in accordance with laws?
Can you only see my darkness covered in flaws?

Will you press pause on the steady stream of bodies carted off to cages?
Can you see past the chains and focus on faces?

Can you only hear me, or do you dare to listen?
Does it make a difference if I'm Muslim or Christian?

Do you care if I serve one year or plenty?
Do you care if the nights alone are many?

Do you care that my brother is in the grave?
Or that you have the power to make me a slave?

Your Honor, I'll tame my tongue and temper as I leave this court with
a rhetorical question:

Can you make the single shot at saving a life your best one?

WHAT MY SON SAID

Hey Dad, I don't wear diapers anymore. I wear pull-ups now.

Dad, I wear big boy underwear now. I don't even pee in the bed anymore.
I went to pre-school today. Dad, did you know that I'm in Kindergarten now?

I can write my name now. I know my letters too.
I can ride a bike now. Mom taught me. I wrecked and scraped my knee.
I cried a little bit.

I'm in the first grade now. I passed. Now I'm in second.
I'm 7 years old now. I had another birthday party. You missed it.

My uncle came and gave me a lot of dollars in all the pockets
of a coat he got me. He talked about you.

I play football, Dad. I play baseball, Dad.

I stole second base. Stealing is not always bad. I'm fast, Dad.

I'm in the third grade now. I passed the
Second grade. It was easy.

Hey Dad, did you know that I'm left-handed sometimes
and sometimes I can use my right one?

I play Basketball. When are you gonna come see me play?

I like to swim.
I like Michael Jackson's music.

I'm smart, Dad. I made A's and B's on my report card.

Outside the Margin of Error

I'm 9 years old now. I got into a fight at school and the Boys-n-Girls Club. I cussed at my teacher.

I passed my reading test. I'm good at reading.

I got in-school suspension. I got suspended. Again.

I told my teacher I want to
Kill myself. I don't. I had to go to the hospital. They asked me
If I want to kill myself. I said no.

I have a game today.
I like You-Tube.

I got in trouble at school Again. I take up for my friends.

The doctor gave mom some pills for me. They make me feel funny.

I made mom cry.

I remember seeing you once. You had a beard. Mom cried. Do you remember?

People say I look like you.

I'm ten years old now. Granny Called. Mom didn't answer.
You called. Mom didn't answer.

Mom's friend spent the night.
He slept beside mom. I think Mom is mad at you. What did you do?
I'm almost done with fourth grade. It's easy.

I got your letter
Hey Dad, when are you coming home?

AN INSIDE LOVE

I believe you made some promises that you can't keep.
You selfishly sought my heart at a time when it came cheap.
It was safe for you to do so, the scales were uneven.
No pain waited for you, only I'd be left with the grievin'.

I was a departure from your past love episode
Looking to change my player ways and live by a different code.
There was no chance I harm, hands around your neck to choke.
No clenched fist to your face. No open-handed smack,
Only the utmost respect for I couldn't go wrong with that.
No chance I cheat or stray because of my present situation.

You were taking advantage of a vulnerable man's incarcerations
Recently ending a long-term relation
Opening up to you about my vow of dedication
That I was ready to pledge to the next queen in my life,
Told you how I would honor her and thank God she was my wife.

My words tickled your ear of course
What woman wouldn't want to hear that my new course
Would place her on a throne as God's greatest creation
And garner her proper praise and celebration?
But I warned you that my current situations
Is not normal for a man doing time.
I told you in the future there may be no phone and not online.
No video chats and no post on Facebook,
No daytime emojis or shower-pix for your eyes to look.

I told you that there would be a time
When the calls were only 15 minutes at a time
And the way we communicate would need your words on paper lines.
You would have to sit still and write down what you think,
Reaching out old-fashioned with pen, paper, and ink.

Told you there would be days or even weeks when we may not speak.
I knew these coming times would try you and expose if you're weak.

Outside the Margin of Error

I warned you to stay away but you assured me that this you chose,
lucky for me, I kept part of my heart closed.

Because I knew I was your rebound, your stories told reveled
your condition
And I allowed myself to believe I was in a strong emotional
position –
But I wasn't.
So the man in me doesn't
Blame you because, more often than not, women are caught up in
their feelings.
I'm just upset with myself for falling victim to such dealings.
I had high hopes, prancing around telling my guys that now I'm
in love with you
But you got put to the test unexpectedly when I went to the S.H.U
Who would have knew
That the ink in your pen was dry or that your stamps weren't
sticky
Or that you couldn't put love in action when our times got tricky.
Please don't feel guilty.

I know in your mind the reasoning behind your actions make all
the sense.
You didn't know that your "I love you's" couldn't follow me
behind the fence.

Just know that I always knew what you meant.
That you loved me because way back we go,
That you loved me because my words made you glow.
Because no man ever greeted you with "good morning queen",
Because my ears listened to how other men treated you mean.
You loved me because I smiled big when your face was in view
And because as old as our friendship was, our love was brand new.
Because my sincerity was real and I was honest about how I fell
I was blunt and kept it real and we have a level playing field.

Outside the Margin of Error

But you felt so much love not because of me
But because of what you didn't see.
The face of the man that bruised your eye, the one that told you lies.
The man that you put to shame,
The man that caused you pain, but it's not you I blame.
It's me, because I knew better, I told you so,
I knew where inside love takes a man, I knew where not to go.
Now part of me is glad because your absence bails me out of my weakness.
And I'll be sure to avoid an inside love again because I know it cuts the deepest.

Lastly, I'll hold on to and cherish our friendship the most
And forever reminisce on the short time you were my lonely loves host.

THEY CALLED OUT TO ME

Voices of my progeny linger, lasting many moments in my lobe.
My ears have captured the faint cry of my offspring.
My senses are heightened; however, I am numb in this cold.
I call out to my seeds which have grown out of my presence and
beyond my grasp. No response.

I call out again, more forcefully this time, straining my chords. Again, no response.
I sit motionless. Listening to the wind hoping to hear a call, a
beacon, a whimper, any sound.

There it is, "Dad, Dad, where are you?"

I respond "Here, I'm right here" now frantic and frozen in place, afraid to move because I'm
afraid to lose the only chance I may have to see their face.

Again, I hear " Daddy, Daddy!" It's
Louder now. My... my child is yelling for me. Fear rest on me now.
Worry has washed over my face. In place, I turn, looking quickly
in each direction, listening harder.

I call back, "Can you hear me?!"

Nothing. No response. I whisper to God, "No. No. No.
Please don't let them be hurt. Please God, please." I ask, "Will
You bring them to me?

"Let me save them. Let me protect them.
Let me be their father, their figure.

Outside the Margin of Error

Please God, bring them into my vision"
God replied, "My son, I will answer your prayers when you awake
from this dream and return home from prison."

FOOT TRAFFIC

Laps on the track they paced beside one another
Spilling beans and guts bonding as brothers

Shuffling left then right then left again
Arms swaying in sync as they slice through wind
It may seem normal but their gait behind the gate is anything but.

You see, society has a blade with which it cut both men deep.
They were mere dots on dominoes that kept fallin'
Till ol' Justice came callin'
They had rights to speedy trials but who wants to hasten an execution?
Some things are normal, but this is anything but.

In the fogs last layers between the suns rise and stars demise
These almost-brothers lamented their circumstances as the rest of
the world moved on with busy lives.
As fast as they find themselves moving around, they just can't keep up.
Normal? Anything but.

Replaying calls to the outside and perceived slights
from family and friends or something like
Agreeing that they can't wait till this quasi-life ends so they
each can return to the reality of past lives
But they don't know that all they currently see is the blinders backside.

Yeah, anything but normal.

TOMORROW TODAY

What will tomorrow bring?
The same ol', same ol' thing: hoping that some mail I see;
A man's deep voice in a high pitch scream,

The click of handcuffs around one wrist at a time,
Beats on the door as amateur rapper's rhyme,

Distant sounds that prove foreign to my senses,
A longing to return to gen pop. So I can at least see the fences,

Spanish language spoken at a rapid pace,
Orderlies sweeping the tier sporting new black eyes on face,

Beeping beepers and buzzing buzzers, cages slam on repeat,
The clicking on floor from hard plastic shoes on feet,

Counting the amount of times officers come to count me,
Eagerly awaiting my three trays of food for feed,

Standing at the door, it never opens but I stare out the glass,
Reminiscing on the fun time of past that's many years passed,

Outside the Margin of Error

Talking about where we hope to go next, me and my celly,
Sleeping days away, tossing turning, side to side, back to belly,

Pacing the floor: 6 steps that way,
Reading the Bible and Koran: front page this way back page that way,

Push-up, sit-up, push-up, then add some squats,
Hoping for a refreshing shower with water not scalding hot,
Hand-wash my body, my underwear and then my socks,

Stand for count, press my bunk, and close my eyes, my nightly thing,
Looking forward to the next day even though I already know what
Tomorrow will bring.

I KNOW MY RIGHTS

I know my rights.
Created 12/15/1791.
Religion, speech, and press
Assemble, petition and the right to own a gun.

I know my rights.
The right to be secure from unreasonable search and seizure.
The right to be left alone, in pursuit of a life of leisure.

I know my rights.
The right to my fifth
And due process of law.
The right to be paid when they seize my private land for all.

I know my rights.
The right to a speedy trial by jury and for the public to see.
Effective assistance of counsel fighting in court for me.
No unfair fines or excessive bail
Or cruel and unusual punishment if I'm locked in a jail.

I know my rights.
The right to reconstruct what was broken for me.
The right to not be a slave is my thirteenth.
The right to fight the charge of a felony.
Because that's how they'll re-enslaved my progeny.

I know my rights.
The right to vote is Amendment fifteen
But the right was rarely realized till' Dr. King preached his dream.

Outside the Margin of Error

Several acts passed over a hundred year span
Till the right to vote was validated in every black hand.
Now I fight for my Bill of Rights
I take a stand by taking a knee.
March in faith blindly so others can see.
Breaking chains in search of what's free.
Longing for love in the sweet land of liberty.

AGAINST AMERICAN GODS

In a battle for my life against impossible odds
Me vs. The System vs. American Gods

Blind justice is a fable
I pull up a seat at the table

Ready to eat the meal the judge will serve
Seated by my attorney, awaiting punishment they say I deserve.

Speaking for the Government they label me as a menace
Dealing poison to the people, handing down a long sentence.

My attorney remains silent although he had no right
To be at a loss for words while they take my life.

Twenty years or more, career criminal. That's the Governments offer
Unless I wish to assist with a hand-written proffer.

I declined the request. I'm ten-toes down
I gotta rep to protect plus I got family in the town.

Side-eye from my lawyer, a pawn for the court
He must be used to clients of a different sort.

I stand to speak, and the bailiff steps my way
It's my last chance to say what I got to say.

I clear my throat,
"Your Honor, I had some chances to do the right things, but I had many more to do wrong.
The leaders in my life taught me all the words to the wrong songs.

Outside the Margin of Error

They told me I had potential to be great then left it to me to figure out
None had a vision or a plan and none taught me about
The pitfalls that lay ahead, the traps in my path
None were offering an ear when I had questions to ask.

I was in life's deep waters with sharks swimming around
But not knowing how to swim I was destined to drown.

Drug addiction in my family, I sold the same
Now I stand before this court, shackled and stating my name.

Do I beg for mercy? Are you a God or a fair judge?
Do you plan to repeat history just because?

I got kids and they will do this time too
If I go to prison chances are they will replace me in front of you
So what's a judge to do?

Stay with the status quo and send a soul up the river?
Or honor the constitution, find justice, and deliver?

Here I stand as a replica of my forefathers, slaves.
My freedom hangs in the balance in the home of the brave.

I'm ready to close this chapter so my future can begin
Then me and the American God can both atone for our sin.

GOD IN A CAGE

We are the trash of your land
You stash us in small towns past back roads
Burden your taxpayer with our heavy loads.

Feed and clothe me for life or as many nights as I can survive
We are your hidden, the one that you hide.

The voices from living graves
Shiny steel shackles slows the movement of us modern slaves
You say we mis-behaved.

That's debatable
But what's not is the fact that I see the hate in you
In exchange for your demise
Disguised as fear of my rise
You work hard to prevent the turning tide
The sunny rise or the scales' lean to my side.

Within these new plantations
We become the reincarnations

Of ancestors long gone
Learn the truth from true soldiers that you've told us all wrong
We learn that we've been God all along

The particles in me are a part of the earth
And the concrete used to build these walls is what it took for me
to discover my worth

Outside the Margin of Error

The science of a Moor used to reverse your curse
I expose your wretched scheme to fill your purse.

I'm not mad because my knowledge is power
Build my patience waiting on the precious hours...of retribution
Immerse myself in deep study of your laws and constitution
Get to know you well.
You had the nerve to place your plots in books.
You don't know me well.
Never thought I'd take those second looks.

Now to me your aim is plain. I see you on my flank
Still making you rich with my free labor. I expect no thanks
You give me tell-lie-visions. I see you ravage my hood with tanks.

Shoot my families then fly your flag
Arrest all our leaders or what little we had
I suppress my anger because I know it's just too bad
That I can't act on this new knowledge I have.

I can't teach the WISDOM and UNDERSTANDING through this phone on the wall

I can't teach CULTURE and EQUALITY at 15 minutes per call
I can't teach my son he's the GOD of it all
Can't teach my EARTH that she BORNE it all
Can't teach my tribe about our rise and fall.

So, I'll lay in this dungeon. Tried by fire. I BUILD my POWER to fight ya'

Because history, repeating itself again on this land, is
Emphatically now CIPHER.

FELON ME

Upon release life will find a way of reminding us of what's
considered bad about ourselves.

Our peers possess a talent for ensuring that we remember that
although we may laugh and smile with one another there remains
between them and us one glaring difference.

The companies that we will solicit to hire us will see to it
that we identify our status on the applications face.
Our names are irrelevant and akin to a non-factor.
All that we are will be summarized by the check in the box that
certifies us as convicted criminals.

Felonies and misdemeanors will forever be tied to the
definitions of our legacies.
Our brave and free country has dictated that things be as such.

The sweet blossoms of rehabilitation that so many close to us
expect to witness will only sprout if we water the planted seeds
of change on the inside while on the inside.

With seemingly insurmountable odds stacked so high against us
we will never be able to afford the cost of being down on
ourselves.

DOORS

Today at Allenwood I saw…
doors closing, slamming, pushed with anger.
Slammed. Locks were turned. Men were restrained.
The bang of the loud slam of the door startled me.
I wanted peace.

I saw doors closed gently;
Doorknobs turned prior to closing to prevent the click of the latch.

DOORS. DOORS. DOORS.

On hinges. Turning. Swinging. Always opening. Never opening.
Retaining a mystery on the other side.

I'm not allowed past its threshold. Doors missing.
Naked hinges with no mate. Scuffed paint and tiles.
Doors off-balance. Is there a door for this cage?
Never a door without a lock. I don't have keys.
No deadbolts, just death.

Big locks. Big keys. Big doors.
Heavy. Wide. Windowless. With windows. Barless. With bars.
Redundant doors. Deterrent.

DOORS. DOORS. DOORS.

Outside the Margin of Error

Cut in half. Top Swinging. Bottom Swinging.
Squeaking doors. WD-40. Oil. Lubricate.

Germs. Don't touch the doors.

Signs on doors directing you to more doors.

DOORS. DOORS. DOORS.

Enter. Exit.

BUIRED ALIVE

Under the rubble of American justice, I lay.
Doomed to the tombs of where I stay.

Processed and politicized, a play imperfect.
Commodified and minimized, invested, made worthless.

Under the towers of trade statues crumble on my head.
Policies pounding away like steel that forms my bed.

I hear white hats and bucket lines as I peek from beneath the pile
Wondering if ever anyone will again see my once-bright smile.

Under color of law red tape forms limestone layers
A thirteenth amendment slave unfreed by mama's prayers.

Somebody come for me. I'm pleading out for help.
Am I just another face at the bottom of the well?

I'm merely existing in this carceral state,
A zip code not hard to find.
Reincarnated as property of state,
Not dead but buried alive.

THIRD STRIKE

On my third strike,
No balls and no foul
I'm down for my life,
My lawyer threw in the towel.

I've been led astray
Like a lamb led to slaughter
Now an absentee parent
To my son and my daughter.

Name and number on paper
Wadded up in the trash.
But worth millions to many,
Traded on Wall Street for cash.

Heartless judges count us out
Then send us away
To languish forever
Life with no release date.

I'll die inside
After I'm dead inside.
So much pain I hide
With my precious pride.

Sunup to sundown
Nights merge into day.
Ruined in some rural town
I'm simply wasting away.

My innings cut short.
I never left home plate.
A minor league player
I never reached first base.

On my third strike. Another swing and a miss.
My life ending before it started. Who ever imagined this?

FAKE NEWS REALITY

At mercy of state,
Vulnerable and exposed
these, these people, these things,
non-believers, no respecter of man...

Behind prisons gate
I should have been safe
protected from the onslaught
of Wuhan lab origins

But this was not my fate
for I am now playing host
to a virus that rented space
in my body like AirBnB

But I am an inmate
How did I come in contact
and become acquainted
with a killer of millions?

I've been infected by state
actors on behalf of bureau
that brought fake news to me
making deadly assaults on my reality.

RECYCLE

Blacks sell crack. Whites sell ice.

Blacks get stopped by the cops.

Blacks resist. Whites resist.

Blacks get beat by the cops.

Blacks go to prison. Whites go home.

The cycle never stops.

TO YEARN

Please,
don't you
dare leave me
in these tested times
plagued with prolonged pandemic problems.

I
am leaning
on you, lost
without you, longing to
Be safely secured to you

We"
holds me.
"We" assures me.
"We's" my silenced sound.
"We" is my sweet solace.

Alone
is not
my humble abode.
Alone is not the
song to be sang aloud.

Venting
sans ventilation,
fearful of meeting
fates of my peers.
Don't you dare leave me.

CELLULAR HOME

My day begins
with the flicker of lights
to cease the prior night.
I feel the effects but lack all control.

From wall to wall I pace.
I lay, and I rise.
I flush, and I wash.
Never venture I beyond rim as fish in a bowl.

CONCRETE ROSE

The rose that grows through concrete

Becomes withered by the weather.

Rain, snow, and unbearable heat;

The fact that it grew many feet

And slipped through

Cracks in concrete

Is only unbelievable to you

For you are the many not the few

You are not he who

Has faith like mustard seed.

Blurred vision won't allow you to see

That the rose that grows from concrete ...is me.

THIS IS US

Young boys, stolen adolescence
Mis-Diagnosed in therapy sessions
Broken homes taught bad lessons.

This is us.

Young girls touched and molested
Pimped out and Dis-Respected
No time spent, and none invested.

This is us.

Ostracized and stigmatized
Criticized and De-Humanized
Deemed unworthy and Uncivilized.

This is us.

Cast into caves without release dates
Locked behind doors with strange cellmates
The ones you feel free to hate.

This is us.

FREE TIME

Time.
Prison.
Free.
Twas given to me.
Argue the fee.
Tax payee.
Time.
Cost
But free when taken from me.
Who is free indeed, me or thee?

CYCLE

Better to die free
Than live as slave
Or spend more time
Inside steel cage

They chain our boys
At tender age
Then turn them loose
In prisons maze

Feed them thrice
And blur their eye
Provide them vice
Until they die

They walk the track
Till hair goes gray
Some buried alive
Forever stay

IN ARBERRATIONS MIDST

All hope abandon ye who enter here!

No more can change
for the better arrive
None shall exit
this desolate wasteland alive

These canyons are grand
& lost in this landscape you shall be
Suns shall rise
& you shall not see

And what has always been shall no more be

Your spirits will be carved
away as terrain with maniacal zeal
The torrent of happiness once possessed
now a meandering trickle into field

Soaking into soil under desert heat
Hot enough to boil too hot for ones feet

IN WAYWARD TIMES

Tied to a stake. Eviscerated.
Eaten by judicial savages
Ensconced in this hellish setting
On a loop in a cell.

Witnessing liberty become supper
The gnashing teeth, white talons dripping
With remnants formerly known as freedom.

Yearning and yelps go unheeded, uncared for, un-

Footage rolling endlessly
Too senselessly

Me and this justice don't share common definitions
A shattered, broken, wasted, nothing
A shell of an unmendable mind

A hollow cavern of hopelessness
Now subservient, a crushed soul
Suspended in some reality.

HOME DECOR

That door: impenetrable, solid
Its glass: unbreakable,

That table: steel, bolted
Its seat: movable, useful,

That shower: tall, boxy
Its water: harsh, unfiltered,

That toilet: soiled, toxic
Its sink: draining, unpredictable,

That bunk: rigid, unforgiving
Its mattress: used, flat

That floor: raw, untiled
Its color dim: dark.

That window: frosted, sealed
Its view: covered, blurry,

This SHU: alive, preying
Its purpose: deadly, accomplished.

RED PILL OR RED PILL

Get tough on crime, declare war on my hood
Pass new laws claiming to be for my good

Turn your cops to soldiers, put tanks on our streets
Cops kill kids then sleep under sheets.

The kids do too but at the hands of foes
New style bracelets as tags on toes

If we stay alive then it's cuffs on wrist
Bruise my body if I squirm and twist

Shout code words like don't resist,
Then with a closed fist you bust my lips.

Before your lords place a price on my head
I can't pay to play so it's three hots and à bed

Take me to your gods, take years from my life
Written in your laws, you think it's right
This pressure on the weak makes them scream at night
But me, I fight.

I live with a dime; I live with a dub
You soaked me in rain, but I swam in the flood

Buried alive but I rise above
You trade life sentences for selling some drugs.

I copped to your offer; the other choice was worse
There are no second chances if I ride in a hearse.

JUVENILE LIFE

I witnessed those young boys.
Those young Black boys
6 to 12 years old
Chained at the neck. Naked
Being led to auction.

Did the price they fetch ever meet the price they paid?
Those young negro males?

Shuffling.
Dirty.

Property, Profit. Unprotected; Insured.
Led through the center of town
Around the circle and to the square
On a hot summer's day, 100 degrees of wrong.

Mothers weep in silence.
Fathers grieve in solitude
Siblings sob without solace.

Those pure Black Bodies.

Beaten.

Grinded to dust into the land.
I witnessed those young negro males
Walking together. Connected.
But not holding hands.

THE ABYSS

Unlock these doors and allow me to escape
Behind barbed wire being chased by hate

Plagued by rage
Freedom's been denied. I'm trapped in a cage.

Walking around in circles, a zombie on the land
Lost in this abyss, no prints in the sand

These are the days of our lives
Prepaid calls to children and wives
Success unseen and locked away for my tries
Tears don't drip. Inside I Cry

My son was a baby and now he's a king
My daughter was a baby and now she's a queen

Lover all alone, no shoulder to lean
All this pain for selling dope to fiends

But what about cigarettes causing cancer deaths
Or D.U.I. alcohol, .08 the breath
Prescription drugs with deadly side effects
My hypocritical homeland does it best

Outside the Margin of Error

Deadbolts on my door, throw away the key
Refused to color in your lines now I'm lost at sea
Missing from the masses, nobodies looking for me
How can I emerge from this new slavery?

SIDE OF THE GLASS

Family torn apart, left my home in shambles
Skating around town on simplistic scrambles

Government cheese aroma lingered in my nose
Tried to change the scent with choices I chose

Pills or crack, grams, or triple stacks
Coke and weed, never needed a strap

Streets were safe in my town. I slept good in bed
Never thought I would daydream in the FEDS

Line up for food, spread my cheeks and cough
Can't control when the lights turn off

Or when they turn on – I'm not in charge
Lost in court to an unbeatable charge
Past life gone away so, so far

Kids grown up with low respect for Dad
Wives moved on. Memories fade fast

You offer good words "Trouble don't last"
That's easy for you to say on the other side of the glass.

STATISTIC

I have been jobless then jailed
Homeless and nailed.

My rates are higher
Last hired first fired.

My babies die more
Their mothers do too
More of me in prison
More of me than you.

I die on the front lines
War on Covid, war with a gun
Crabs out the bucket sometimes
Police kill just for fun.

Ball in your hoop
Graceful moves on court
Trapped in justice loop
Grace un-given in court.

A project incomplete
The projects where I sleep
The worst view I see
Freedom ain't free for me.

TRUE BILL

What does justice mean?
Hands behind backs or cuffs on wrist?
Juvenile life or lethal injection?
Come on, no way it means this.

Constitution. Institution. Retribution.

Justice by geography
Who knows the lay of the land?
Map out the system. Topography.
Incarcerate the races of man.

Constitution. Institution. Retribution.

Courthouse. Jailhouse. White House. Outhouse.
The symbols of American shit
One truth is self-evident:
Liberty and justice for all is just a myth.

Constitution. Institution. Retribution.

Freedom ain't free.
Freedom is on sale for cash.
Freely close your eyes and see.
Freedom is based on class.

Constitution. Institution. Retribution.

WHAT A GIFT

Beyond the fence and beyond the gate
New worlds exist and my future waits

My clock ticks down and calendars lose pages
I was servant of my sins now sentenced to pay wages

Courtrooms and clerks, appeals getting denied
Anger boiling at informants who lied

Missing many birthdays and days when family died

The sunshine is not the same on this side of the wall
I've traveled through this maze, bounced around like a ball

A pawn on the board in life's game of chess
Sharing this experience with fellows east to west

Lockdowns and count every day on repeat
I'm just something forced to stand on my feet

Or made to sit in a seat
Some choose to pray on a knee

Blow trial or cop to a plea
I was given a lot of time somehow good and bad for me
One thing's for sure is that this gift of time was not free

WITHOUT LIBERTY

In confinement we exist without liberty;
Victimized by this culture of division that enriches
itself on the pains of the people that are presently
pushed to the margins of this world.

OPERATOR

You have a prepaid call from...
An inmate at a Federal Prison.

There they stand
Behind a gate
Bearing the weight;
Dialing in amongst cast-outs
To see if you listen.

Your dad.

An inmate at a Federal Prison.

Press 7 to reject
Or better yet
Press 5 to accept.
Talk with your old man.
Make something he won't forget.

Memories.

Press 7 to reject
or better yet
Press 5 to accept.

It's your decision.

You have a prepaid call from... your dad.

An inmate at a Federal Prison.

S.H.U.MILIATION

Step in there.
Take off all your clothes. Yes, all of them.

Everything.
Throw them on the floor in the corner over there.

Face me.
Lift your arms.
Spread your fingers.
Open your mouth.

Wider!
Stick out your tongue.
Move it left. Move it right. Lift it.

Lift your penis.
Lift your sack.
Turn around.

Let me see the bottom of your left foot. Your right one.
Spread your cheeks.
Squat and cough.

What size pants, shirt, and underwear for you?
Don't worry, we already know – this is the right size S.H.U.

BAND OF BROTHERS

For all we know we may never see each other again
So let's chisel our presence into the bricks

Be in this moment together as captives within
Stamp our memories so the pain sticks.

A band of brothers fighting gods of injustice
In these trenches our bonds become tight

America will soon have to uncuff us
In a free field of battle we'll continue this fight.

The leaders of our tribes, our destiny awaits
Past victims of circumstance

Wisdom from journeys written on face
Sand of time passes through hands

Prisoners of war, no rescue team in route
Our freedom depends on inside help

This battle for life, a heavyweight bout
We'll take our liberty by the power inside self.

KNOCKING AT MIDNIGHT

There was a knock at midnight
And you answered the call
A goddess in disguise
A savior sent to soften the fall.

Our hero at ground zero
Policies poisoned our hood
But you returned to the people
Giving glad tidings of good.

Held down in holes
Our lives lived in shame
But you knew of the life
On the other side of the game.

Our parents chasing dragons
Washing worth down the drain
Terrible traumatic transitions
Prison yard to yard pulling chain.

Holding on to hope
When chains on black flesh we see
Negativity in Newsweek
Publish perp walk pictures of me.

The lost are looking to be found
To unlock doors of peace
A closer proximity to freedom
Is what bolsters their belief

Girls embracing mothers
After judges grant pleas for mercy
But decades before
The same judges deemed mothers unworthy.

But God is a mighty God!
The creator knows the heart.
So the steppers step past midnight
As the new dawn represents a new start.

COLOR GUARD

I followed a new paradigm and became a paragon;
Lessons learned from those of past times: from Garvey to
Malcom to Martin to Farrakhan.

My changed thinking has led to this new path I am now on.
I was labeled a flight risk then denied bond.
Served a long sentence and still considered a con
And that's something less than a man
Because society will never take me back.
This is a life-long harvest because I planted my seeds with cocaine-crack.

This world shows no mercy and definitely cuts no slack,
Offers no forgiveness and only a semblance of a second chance.
They throw us off the boat in deep waters with no extension of a helping hand
But I think I can, I think I can.

I'm the little engine that could.
Made a pariah amongst my peers for simply doing what I thought
Should
Be done, that's pursuing this mirage of an American dream for
a little fun in the sun

But my fast life turned to a fast run
Then I ended up missing the entire life of my son.
Lord have mercy!!, what have I done?

How can I bounce back like round ball
After bouncing up to my feet night after night just to satisfy
the institutional roll call?

C'mon y'all, we lost and looking for answers.
While our brothers and sons are getting murdered in the streets
our sisters and daughters are taking dollars as dancers
We pulling the sled of second-class citizens like Rudolph and Prancer.
This mind-state has metastasized like a malignant tumor... Cancer.

We gotta break free from the bondage of the bling-bling.
Lift every voice to high-heavens and sing-sing
From the rec. yards of Camp Fed to S.H.U at the U.S.P.

Outside the Margin of Error

What a thing-thing it will be
To take a stand or take a knee
Or be remembered as a revolutionary
Because every one of them in history
Had hands cuffed and freedom stripped but that was just a fee
That had to be paid so the path could be paved
To teach the next man the proper way to behave
In a way that means more than living life just to get paid
I'm afraid

My brothers are in the mirror grooming their waves, braids,
locks, and fades
Only seeing the reflection of a handsome thirteenth amendment slave
What a shame... how we chased those dollars, but it didn't make sense
And the prosecutor solicits a sentence that defies common sense

And so easily steal our freedoms with no plans for recompense.

I see no mercy over yonder in the hearts of Trump and Pence.
What 's my fifteen when I got brothers and sisters that's
gonna die behind the fence?

So it's my duty to be a force beyond the fence
And lead the charge past the gate;
To slap a smile on the face of a felon before he meets his fate.
I'm eager to carry the flag and be the one to advocate

And be the voice for the plight of the unknown brother and
sister behind bars, walls and fences doing time
Who had to reap the wrath of the American prison industrial
complex and learn the hard way that that lady justice...
she was never blind.

COMPOUND INTEREST

Let's have a conversation about what's complex, I'm talking about
the prison industrial,
Warehousing human flesh, killers, kings, convicts, and fathers
non-custodial.
Psychological warfare, tough on crime policy, Nixon-era politics
reign supreme,
Never harmed the hair on the head of a human but destined to die
in prison for chasing a dream.

We're on the DOW 30, traded publicly on the Wall Street exchanges
If ever questioned about such a diabolical scheme Congress would
refuse to explain this.
Prisons for profit, C.C.A.. Geo Group, selling beds just to meet a
quota
ADX in the side of a mountain to camp FED in Yankton, South Dakota
Nose in the spine of a book, getting smarter while getting older.

Tired of washing clothes in a toilet bowl, cheap bar of soap in
my hand,
Haven't felt the touch of a woman in many years, been making love
to my hand.
I bet you never heard the screams like those of a man being raped
by man
Looking in the mirror trying to convince the reflection that that
man is still a man.

Earning a G.E.D. is a thrill to some. I've seen guys cheer then
engage and embrace,
Prison politics conquer the yard, can't talk to my friend because
it's a race vs. race. What a waste
Of manpower, labor, taxpayer money although some guys do here

belong,
Young boy told me he never tasted a woman. He ain't ever going home.
What could he have done that was just so wrong?

Tobacco, weed, deuce and tunchi, sugar, bread, and wine
Come with a year and a day but now doing a dime for petty crime.

Lock in a sock, toothbrush for a knife, beat a man with a cane
Appeals get denied, pushing down the floor just to cope with pain.

Here's the epitome of shame:
Bastards raping babies or selling pics and they only get a year,
But 10 grams sold, 50 year sentence my partner never shed a tear.
Where's the justice and equality?
Examples of injustice simply boggle me
Come behind this fence so you can follow me
Imagine the pain when I know my child is screaming, calling me.

Tickets and tattoos. Food out the kitchen, tru-lincs to MP3s
Walking miles on the track daydreaming and scheming in the breeze
Pursuing degrees and PhDs

How about a little history please:
Reagan's D.A.R.E. Program, Just Say No! The Sentence Reform Act
Then Clinton built more prisons
Our Government has no regrets about the effects of its past decisions

To sentencing commissions, guideline time, Kimbrough, Booker, all drugs minus 2,
Fair Sentencing Act, Smart on Crime Policy, Obama clemency freed my dude,
Mathis, Descamps, Johnson, and Havis. Some got trapped and some made it through.

I swear faces disappear like water flows down the drain,
Waking up every morning, every day is just the same. Prison time don't change.
They told me to just be patient, do my time, all things work out.
Well tell that to the man with a life sentence that's never walking out.
Fuck what you talking about!

Man on his knees praying to God, fighting evil policies devised by man,
You'd be hard pressed to convince him that this is God's divine plan.

Outside the Margin of Error

He shall forever remain nameless, an inmate, a number, a grain of sand
The A.P.R. on the yard may many times fluctuate.
Up and down from date to date,
There will never be an easy way for you to calculate
the compound interest.

VENTILATION

Many times I feel there is no exit to prisons maze,
Checking my watch, watching the calendar, counting the days.

All around my brothers are blind, ignorant of the way,
Not mindful of their ways
Twisting up dreads or brushing down the waves,
Rocking du-rags, living in a daze;
No matter if you got a bald head or tight-ass fade
In time the mirror you see the reflection of a cute ass slave,
A grown ass coward in the home of the brave.

I know my words are extreme but that's the song that I plays.
I'm on a quest for knowledge to be wise beyond my age,
We can never kneel with Kaepernick if we don't read the words on the page,
Take a radical approach to change and engage.

How can you do all this time and remain unchanged?
I'm simply amazed at how you remain unfazed
And the saddest part of all is that even upon release you'll remain in a cage.

Because instead of education you went outside and played,
Could've abandoned your past life but you chose to stay,
Steady chasin' a dollar to get rich and paid
Instead of creating a legacy to be remembered as great.

You see, Martin moved with caution, but Malcom couldn't wait
For good ol' America to offer some crumbs off the plate.
We should have been free out the gate.
Now itchy-finger cops determine our fate.

Outside the Margin of Error

Our civil-rights leaders slept with the devil on the first date.
Decades later we still got hooks in our mouths because they took
the bait.

Some say change will come soon but soon may be too late;
Such a waste of good anger if you hear my words and scrunch your face.

We hunger for the best of life, but we can't fathom the taste,
We took the wrong routes with heroin and cocaine-base.

Now you pay attention when slim shady got something to say?
You sleep with a double decade and refuse to study your case,
Get the fuck out of my face!!

You're on a one-way street to becoming a disgrace
To your family and your race;
You looking at life thru broken windows but thinking it's cool
because the curtains are lace.

Our culture is most imitated and emulated but remains in last place.
Churches chicken in the church while our daughters are being raped
By the Pastor's son that's living the lyrics of the song he plays on the tape.
You love loving lesbians but gay men you hate.
What kind of double standard did we create?

It's time to clean the slate.
We chase ice without first learning how to skate.
You want to understand why we kill each other? It's because hatred,
for my brother is baked into the cake.
But the icing was just so sweet that we loved every bite we ate.

BRANDED

This conviction don't make me.
I stood ten-toes with the judge, faced 25 and he still couldn't
break me.
But I've seen those so-called gangsters fold like dollar bills
and that aint fake news that's just a fake 'G'

You see, I live by a code, that's a set of principles that define my beliefs.
And I'm going to stick to my guns till I can turn my mothers'
grief to relief or at least bring her peace.

You see, I've seen rooms full of life turn deadly
at the same time.
It was a shame I Was so cold-hearted that my money meant more than your life
at the same time.

I didn't give a damn about mine or my own kind;
People who look just like me
Would sell me their soul for a hit off the pipe then act like
they like me, but it's highly likely
They were just chasing a pipe dream
And I loved it, on to the next fein;

Mother, son, father, daughter, pastor, and priest,
They all made the call. To say the least in the streets I was a
beast.
But I've seen death return to the grave. To money I was a slave,
Beholden to the benefits, no damn I gave.
To hell with you if you opposed how I behaved.

Outside the Margin of Error

I was out to get rich by any means and many schemes.
I'd sell you the pills, coke, crack, weed or even a pistol to
help you shoot down your own dreams.
What you mean how could I? Why would I? Did I ever ask myself should I?
Man, for that dollar I'd poke out your good eye.
But to my family who loved me, I was Mr. Good-guy,

To the women who touched me I was Mr. Too-fly,
Quick to tell two lies
I Kept some good dope so you know my feins kept a good high.

But truth be told, I was a cold piece of shit,
Sometimes lower than the ground on which you spit.
And pops wasn't around so pops never taught me shit.

And it's many more just like me
You might have, and you might not see
A changed man I might and I might not be.
Why the FEDS had to pick a fight with me?

The constitution says I got the right to life but why I never
had the chance to have one?
A prison sentence where I'm from is like low-hanging fruit so I
just reached up and grabbed one.

We were doomed from the start, have you seen the numbers? They
may vary a little depending on your class
But when you're born into American poverty the system don't mind
hiding your...

Ask me a question and I'll tell you the facts
You may fare a little better as long as you're just not black
But even I was born with this light skin and they didn't cut me
no slack. So, what's up with that?
Now I stand in front of you as the true definition of a stat.

So now we got the new Jim Crow aka the D.O.J. They're the real
lock-em-up type.
And no offense to my caucus of Caucasians but we know the leader is white.

But don't get it twisted, he'll lock up any type:

Outside the Margin of Error

Nigger, honkey, jew, engin, spic, or kite. That's what he likes.

So if you think for one second when you walk in the streets it's
going to be all good your ship must not be sailin'
Because you've been branded with a scarlet "F" on your chest and it stands for
convicted felon.

ANOTHER SAD SONG

There is no artist that can paint a picture that depicts what drugs do to the community.
Most of us hustlers lived like it was only you and me

Because that's just how it was, a rat race so fine.
Capitalism is just so def, dumb and blind

To the plight of the user and their families alike.
I've never sold a racist drug, it welcomes black, brown and white

To roll up, shoot up, drink up and snort
The effects can't be measured by any court ordered report.

Paperwork doesn't help us understand why in the back alley:
someone's daughter is dropping to her knees
All that matters is if I can get a good price on the keys

I've seen the zombies on the floor in the middle of the night
crawling around looking for crumbs of crack,
I continued to smoke my weed and get a good laugh at that.
But lo and behold if your mother did that. Now laugh at that.

You know someone that texted, sexted, went to rehab to be
corrected but to no avail.
Loss of a job, family, and self-respect. Finally sober in jail, what the hell?

People pass by food, pass over money, and pass off their children
for a hit off the pipe
Then go home and avoid the mirror because they can't stand the
sight.

Outside the Margin of Error

I might Have been that person, but my drug was the dollar.
I had the nerve to consider myself better than those who consume my product.
Then before a judge I failed to justify my conduct.

Did I care if people quit jobs, lost homes, or chose a life in foreclosure?
Or had the fortunes of a tattered four-leaf clover?
Hell no ten-times over!!

The spiral downward is hidden by smiling faces, meth-mouth and rotting flesh.
Finally hitting rock bottom, the zombie apocalypse looking like walking death. It takes my breath

To know I contributed to the destruction of mankind
Just for some nice clothes, a fancy car and some damn shine.

I was the one that was sick and diseased and purely rotten to my core
But my good friend, greed, kept me pushing for more.

Truth be told, I needed some rehab, I needed some hustlers' remorse
Because I would have destroyed more lives had I stayed the course

Of course, my kids had nice things and saw our bills get paid
But also saw S.W.A.T. kick in the door, daddy in cuffs led away after raids
Did I really have it made?

The former junkie has recovered, now at home making a life with their kids.
I got three with no daddy. So you tell me what gives?

Nothing, that's what.

I'm waiting for the chance to rectify my wrong.
I'll live to a different tune next time and never live the lyrics to another sad song.

FREE TILL I'M FREE

I won't be free till I'm free
Even when the system has mileage and acres set aside for me
Or even when I'm in the woods where none can see
Tip-toeing the perimeter or in the garden planting food to eat
The fact remains: I'm not free till I'm free.
There may be no cell, not barbwire fence or bars for me
No strip down after visit and family come more frequently
With social media in my palm and the latest movies to see
The simple fact remains: I'm not free till I'm free.

Sure the U.S.P. is the worst
And the F.C.I. better than where some start at first

Living the low life is better than both and Lord knows the camp
was just too sweet
But it never felt quite right because I'm not free till I'm free.
I had a bunk to myself and no man slept over top of me,
I had four lockers filled with stuff and commissary to eat,
Only had one C.O. for 90 men, I barely heard the keys
But at 9pm. the doors locked. More evidence I wasn't free.
At 4pm still I had to stand to my feet
And at 12, 3, and 5a.m. the flashlight shined bright on me.
I saw lobster tail and ate shrimp scampi from the sea
But I had to duck and hide because I still wasn't free.
Many may read my words or hear my voice and form an opinion about me
But I'm just living in my truth realizing that I'll never be free till I'm free.

I met guys in the penn with 40 points when I only had 11, neither of us could leave
And when I told them about the camp they just couldn't believe.
Motorola, 2 Galaxies, and a Z.T.E., even had access to the new L.G.
Till I got knocked and ended up in the S.H.U. at U.S.P. Lee.
The biggest reminder of all that even at the camp I wasn't free.

I drove a John Dere, a Ford Ranger and the new F-150,
Could have left for hours and no one would miss me
Could have went to the hotel, had the ol' lady come get me,
But I never left for hours and never had her see me
Facing escape charges. Again, not free till I'm free.
As you go to low security, they expect you to act grateful at least

Outside the Margin of Error

But truth-be-told they only extend you a longer leash
Saying they protect the public because I and you are beast
And use unjust laws to withhold our freedom and peace.
That's not my kind of free.

At the camp they threaten to send you back to the low, behind the
fence. From the low to medium and from there to the U.S.P.
But to a man, a real man, it doesn't matter where you send me
because I'll never be free till I'm free.

HABITUAL OFFENDER

These are the seven habits of the highly effective.
They may serve as surefire ways to help you meet many objectives,
So please, be selective.

HABIT #1: Be proactive. That means to act in anticipation of a
problem or a need.
One thing you can anticipate is your problem being
your greed.
An unquenchable desire for more and more, a need, to
get high or a need to score.
So act in advance in hopes of decreasing your fail rate
Because no man-made plan contains a fail-safe.

***HABIT #2*:** Begin with the end in mind.
Now that we know life is a marathon, we should be inclined to take our time.
Because how you commence is a good indicator of how
you'll complete.
With a recidivism rate of 80% it seems staying free is some great feat.
Staying on my feet seems simple enough to me until the first hint of defeat drops me to my
knee.

HABIT #3: Put first things first.
Now that's self- explanatory
It carries much weight; simply put, get your priorities straight.
Because what's most important is not on my list of wants but on my list of needs.
All over this country there are thousands more waiting to take pleas just like me.

All with the same story of priorities misplaced.
Now we deal with the pain of families displaced,
Praying for our safety in this place.
Paying to come see me in this place.
Mama cries when she sees the look on my face.
What a waste... of a good tear.

HABIT #4: Three simple words: Think win-win.
If positive psychology is the make-up of your biology
then psychologically my friend you've got one foot in.

Outside the Margin of Error

The journey to your future requires your presence in
the present so change from your ways and repent from your sin.
In all your dealing both sides must benefit or else a deal is no deal at all.
They say life is a rollercoaster but we are mere mortals that can only take so much rise and fall.

HABIT #5: Seek to understand then to be understood.
That sounds like a proverb meant to bring some good
So let me knock on some wood. If I could, I would
Live by such a habit that entails putting the next man before myself.
This positive precept can serve as the foundation to my health, long life and wealth.

HABIT #6: Synergize.
This is a principle of creative cooperation.
It starts with something as simple as a conversation,
Joint communication between two parties with a positive
goal in mind. Surround yourself with a network of like minds
That is certain to have your best interest at heart
Because emerging from such a dark place it's critically
important to give yourself the best possible start.

HABIT #7: Sharpen the saw.

Because with a dull blade we can never cut the dead wood.
We must protect our most important asset and act towards our own good:
Our spiritual, physical, social, and mental dimensions.
Striving for our personal best will undoubtedly command our undivided attention.

Wíithout a doubt what lies ahead in life is truly unpredictable,
Second and third chances, you may feel like a beginner.
Without a doubt these seven habits a certainly indispensable
So don't misunderstand when I implore you to become a habitual offender.

ABANDONED

You left me.
In a helpless state there I was
Holding on to you just because
You were all I could grip.
The memories of past have done just that;
Fading away like a taper,
Prayer for her help no to hate her
My path now slick with tears. I have begun to slip.

Your cold shoulder is the coldest that I can recall from recent memory.
I have fought against your negative energy.
I'm stumbling into myself. I have begun to trip.
Something better I've become:
An example for our son.
Possess the spirit of a champion.
I don't quit.

Visions of your exit
Torment my days and shorten my nights.
Glimpses of your face flash in lights.
I spit.
Together we lived.
Also we died.
You rose while I remained.
I'll never forget nor forgive
How you left me alone amongst my worst pain.

FATHERHOOD SLAIN

I'm an unfree father behind the fence but a daddy I remain
Searching for creative ways so that I can effect change
In the blossoming seeds that have sprouted from my loins
Using my comings and goings
As a springboard for life-long lessons to learn.
Hoping to prevent a turn
To resentment and anger toward the absentee parent, that be me.
I've been to court, negotiated visitation and custody of course
for a small fee.

I've settled for weekends and two weeks out of the summer
But what's that compared to not seeing my youngins' for seven
whole summers?
Child support enforcement, guns and badges pulled out in my face
Cuffed up for a perp-walk now I got a case.
Looking back at my children I see a future with no father written
all over their face.
Feelin' like a failure like I can't provide for my own
Two to the dome,
That's what it feels like when they ask on the phone "daddy, when
you coming home?"
I finally come clean and now my covers blown. I've sewn
Some seeds and I hope the fruit ripens to be something better
than me.
I want them to be the best of the best of the best but I'll
settle for the best that they can be.

I gotta learn more so I can teach them the same.
I understand nature has its own way but it's up to me to nurture the brain.

Outside the Margin of Error

Fifteen minutes at a time I believe my words can penetrate;
For a fruitful future it's up to me to initiate

I'll light the spark and ignites the flame,
Prophesy their strength so they can break these chains.
The statistics say they are more likely to come here simply because I came.

Not many words to express my feelings of frustration, shame, pain;
I'll fight with every fiber and grain
Of my being to: ensure their future is better than mine;
Learning to be the father I never had while I conquer my time.
Can I be an influence? Instill values? Culture and character?
Tell me what could be scarier
Than seeing that which you love go astray?
I'm anxiously counting calendars and patiently awaiting my day.

Pictures captured the growth spurts; birthday candles burned
But I only saw them frozen in time.
Someone said there was light at the end of this tunnel
But I'll be damned if I can see the shine.
Whose fault is that? Mine.

I'm he who is to blame
If my son hustles in the game or my daughter is crushed under
the weight of loves pain.
All I can do now is focus on what could be because I killed what
should have came
I'll manage to make more memories to replace this vivid vision
of fatherhood slain.

LEAVING YOU IN THE FIRE

How can some people say that they love us then leave us
especially when they know the pain that we feel?
For some men the only way to know that jail or prison is real is
to be in jail or prison. The fire has to burn us.
Some of us must be left alone, by ourselves, no help, no friends,
no family, nothing. Some of us were just "too cool".

Fast cars, big rims, jewelry, money and most important of all
women, women, and more women. But what if all that stuff was just
not real? What happens when none of those things exist?
What does life look like when a man can't accessorize?
When he's stripped down to his core?

It looks like the inside of a jail cell.
It looks like chow time, and count time, and lock down.
It looks that way for days and weeks and months and years.
It looks that way for birthdays and holidays and New Years and Christmas.
It looks that way for momma and daddy's funeral. For decades.
It looks that way for life.

But for some of us the only way we can finally become the great
men that we are destined to be is to lay in that dungeon, in those
dismal crips. Alone. No love from nobody. No kind words. No hand
reaching out to hold ours. Great men like us need that pain.
The worst pains before we can make the most gains.

Outside the Margin of Error

Lying in that bunk late nights is where you will discover who you truly are. You will never discover who you are meant to be and what you are meant to be while surrounded by the many fish in the sea. Surrounded by mirage-like men that disappear like smoke.

You are where you are because God is making you. You are being prepared for the battlefields. This is your training ground.

The people who really love you know this to be true. The only one to not know is you. They know you need this pain. They can't save you. The prophecy is being fulfilled. You are a man now. This is on you. Don’t fight against them because they see what you cannot, but you will, and when your greatness emerges you will thank them for leaving you in the fire.

SEASON PASS

I received a season pass
To watch the seasons pass.
My lens for life is prisons glass:

A windowpane that restricts my pain from escaping.
I watch the blossoms bloom as life returns to the exterior
While being commanded to sit and stand as if I'm inferior.

What a time this is.

The sun's heat is at work, but I can't feel.
If only I could carve a path past this windows seal
I would happily dance with bare feet in the grassy field

I know the wind is blowing for the spiders' web sways
And I watched ants carry crumbs to prep for future days.
The solar star has cast into my quarters rays
Of life but I don't feel alive.
My only joy is substance provided at p.m. 5.

I'm seeing the seasons pass
Because I have a season pass
To view life through prisons glass.

The leaves of Autumn are pressed to the earth destined to
continue the cycle
That's ever so vital.
The winter months after Fall arrive.
The waters have frozen so now you can't enjoy a dive.

Outside the Margin of Error

I'm laughing at you now. None happier than I.

I've grown bitter as the cold.
The snow falls, and I think 'How can you be so bold
To move about while with this pain behind this pane I remain?'

My logic is lost on you.
My sanify has fled.
A snowflake found my window today and held on to the edge
Before the breeze blew it away. I wonder where it landed.
Does its creator care that I am stranded?

Ice has formed on my lens
And it will melt and be gone before my season ends.
One day soon raindrops will drip before my eyes
And I'll make futile attempts to measure the size
Without understanding the why.
So obstructed is my view that I barely see the sky.

In months to come the flowers will return and again nature
you will enjoy at last.
I will still be viewing through my prisons glass
The seasons pass
In possession of my season pass.

RECENT REMINDERS

Bars on windows block my view
Locks on doors prevent walk-through
Appeals for freedom, I've filed a few
Crossed red lines, spent time in S.H.U.

Waited on mail, no letters landed
Ships set sail, I'm left stranded
Bonds with brothers been disbanded
Cold-hearted comments, made off-handed.

Presidential policies shorten my sentence
Punish my pride, offer repentance
Ordered to shut up, I stop mid-sentence.

Recent reminders, I'm not my own
Reaping a harvest, seeds I've sewn.
Repeat offender, chances blown
Life on papers, living on loan.

A MOMENT OF ESCAPE

I rang your line because I need to hear your voice
You are the relief from the beatdowns of my choice.

I seek solace and peace from the words you speak
Gaining strength from your spirit to complete my week.

How you been? Hows the family? Wife and kids?
I want you to know I'm grateful for the time you give.

Because every time you accept my call it's my moment of escape
We laugh about my life sentence, me not having a release date.

The fact I'm never getting out is never an issue
When we speak the tears don't drip. I don 't need the tissue.

I live through you. I brag about your success.
Elated by your exploits. I'm no longer depressed
Your new house, cars, trucks, and the clothes you wear
Keeps me in the streets and makes me feel like I'm there.

Females on the scene, you let me spit some game
I'll never touch one again; imagine my pain.

This call is about to end. We only got one minute left
Plus the C.O. is looking at me. Let me go before things go left.

I'm glad I got to speak with you and relieve some stress.
You're the realest friend I got. As a matter of fact,
you're the best.

ETCHED IN THE ECHOES

I'm stirred strongly in my soul from haunting echoes of a time passed.
They lived at times, in jubilee despite sorrowful surroundings,
my people.

Bound in bondage they were but ever basking in the stars ray.
Toiling in the day. Soaking in the soul with sweat from furrowed brows.
They sang.

Little children with mother played in the cottons row,
helping at time to lift the bags of golden fleece.
Was it in peace they lived? Mother, father, child held tightly
behind walls high as babel's tower?

Emphatic is the no that trails closely such a rhetorical query.
It is in the midst of turbulent times behind fortress-like walls
that I search for that elusive peace.
Humming the melodies of those haunting echoes
The refrains of resistance I bellow.
No bags of golden fleece I fill
But toil I just the same in field.
Fighting back sorrow in such surroundings.

LOOSEN THE NOOSE

Condemned in a bad situation, in need of intervention
Suppressed and neglected and oppressed not to mention.

Jobs left the city, overseas was the way
People got no pity, change the channel on my day

Politicians in power paid poor folks no mind
Chose to make war on people of my kind:

Gang up on the ghettos, my home the government made
Red lines restricting a good life in the shade.

Turn a blind eye to the dangers of the dope
Another blind eye to Central American coke
Ignoring my despair, it's impossible to cope
Hello to the crack era, goodbye to hope.

Prisons get built and they fill them up with me
Behind high walls it's impossible to see.

I lose in court, but my family does time
Lights out on my future makes it hard to shine.

Teach I'm bad for choosing the life I chose
I study the books and press ‘em close to my nose
Peek into the past to see what history shows
Peel back the layers now the secrets exposed.

The war on drugs is really a government attack
Tough on crime meant to target the blacks
The new Jim Crow to keep a foot on the back
They loosened the noose but now they tighten the slack.

Outside the Margin of Error

I sharpen my blade to do some good in my hood
Now I understand, seek to be understood.

First things first, I got priorities straight
Serve time for the crime now I walk out the gate
Be a force for the people, changing the scene
And teach a new way to chase American dreams.

THE LEFT BEHIND BROTHER

Good brother one day I'll see you again
And we'll laugh at our times in jails and pens.

I remember when your son got sick, and your lady walked away.
Those were some tough times. I remember them like yesterday.

Remember the migos killed the guy from Philly & G.D.'s warred with the Bloods?
The DC boys sayin' "slim" and "mo" and all the Crips sayin' "cuz"?

Remember the Father's Day visits, just us and the kids at the visitation?
Remember I got knocked with the phone and lost six months visitation? -

Remember hours on con-air, shackled hands and feet?
Flying the green mile on the way to OKC?

Remember the slimy greens and baked ziti for chow?
We never got sick though. Only God knows how.

Remember I thought you could really ball?
Remember buying all the fifteen-minute calls?

We made it through lock downs. Had to bathe out of the sink.
I remember you had the loudest farts. Damn they used to stink.

Outside the Margin of Error

We used to wait on a letter
Just knowing time would get better.

We stayed in that cell for almost two months that time
With days like that I'm surprised I didn't lose my mind.

Well good Brother, I was just droppin' you some lines because I can't drop by
Until we meet again, don't Let the time do you and hold your head up high.

APPENDIX

Herein is presented a mosaic of authenticity, interwoven with court documentation and transcripts, prison pay stubs, facility memorandums, and a visual narrative captured through photographs.

These artifacts not only bear witness to my incarceration but also serve as a testament to the spirit of finding expression amidst adversity.

Aaron in 2023 post-incarceration; Augusta, Ga
4Life Photography

Outside the Margin of Error

Change of Plea Transcript

July 2012

1

UNITED STATES DISTRICT COURT
EASTERN DISTRICT OF TENNESSEE
GREENEVILLE

UNITED STATES OF AMERICA, . DOCKET NO. CR-2-10-84
GOVERNMENT, .
VS. . GREENEVILLE, TN
. JULY 25, 2012
AARON KINZER, . 1:28 P.M.
DEFENDANT. .
. . . .

TRANSCRIPT OF CHANGE OF PLEA
BEFORE THE HONORABLE J. RONNIE GREER
UNITED STATES DISTRICT JUDGE

APPEARANCES:

FOR THE GOVERNMENT: U.S. DEPARTMENT OF JUSTICE
OFFICE OF U.S. ATTORNEY
J. GREGORY BOWMAN, AUSA
220 WEST DEPOT STREET, SUITE 423
GREENEVILLE, TN 37743

FOR THE DEFENDANT: LEONARD, KERSHAW & HENSLEY
DAVID L. LEONARD, ESQ.
131 SOUTH MAIN STREET, SUITE 102
GREENEVILLE, TN 37743

COURT REPORTER: KAREN J. BRADLEY
RPR-RMR
U.S. COURTHOUSE
220 WEST DEPOT STREET
GREENEVILLE, TN 37743

PROCEEDINGS RECORDED BY MECHANICAL STENOGRAPHY, TRANSCRIPT PRODUCED BY COMPUTER.

2

(CALL TO ORDER OF THE COURT AT 1:28 P.M.)

THE COURT: ALL RIGHT. MS. HOPSON, WOULD YOU CALL THE FIRST AFTERNOON CASE, PLEASE.

THE CLERK: USA VERSUS AARON KINZER, CASE NUMBER CR-2-10-84.

(DEFENDANT SWORN)

EXAMINATION

BY THE COURT:

Q. MR. KINZER, YOU ARE CHARGED IN EACH COUNT OF A NINE COUNT SECOND SUPERSEDING INDICTMENT RETURNED BY THE GRAND JURY IN THIS CASE. IT IS MY UNDERSTANDING THAT YOU HAVE NOW ENTERED INTO A PLEA AGREEMENT WITH THE UNITED STATES. I AM INFORMED THAT PURSUANT TO THAT PLEA AGREE-MENT YOU WISH TO CHANGE YOUR PLEAS TO PLEAS OF GUILTY AS TO COUNTS 1, 2 AND 9 OF THIS NINE COUNT INDICTMENT, COUNT 1 CHARGING YOU WITH A CONSPIRACY TO DISTRIBUTE 28 GRAMS OR MORE OF COCAINE BASE OR CRACK, COUNT 2 CHARGING YOU WITH A CONSPIRACY TO DISTRIBUTE 50 KILOGRAMS OR MORE OF MARIJUANA AND COUNT 9 CHARGING YOU WITH A CONSPIRACY TO COMMIT MONEY LAUNDERING; IS THAT CORRECT?
A. YES.
Q. ALL RIGHT. BEFORE I CAN ACCEPT YOUR GUILTY PLEAS, THERE ARE A NUMBER OF QUESTIONS I NEED TO ASK YOU TO ASSURE THAT THOSE PLEAS ARE VALID ONES. IF YOU DO NOT UNDERSTAND ANY QUESTION, PLEASE ASK ME TO EXPLAIN IT TO

Outside the Margin of Error

I was classified as a career offender and facing a life sentence due to two prior drug convictions (three strikes).

PART B ¯ CAREER OFFENDERS AND CRIMINAL LIVELIHOOD

§4B1.1. Career Offender

(a) A defendant is a career offender if (1) the defendant was at least eighteen years old at the time the defendant committed the instant offense of con- viction; (2) the instant offense of conviction is a felony that is either a crime of violence or a controlled substance offense; and (3) the defendant has at least two prior felony convictions of either a crime of violence or a con- trolled substance offense.

(b) Except as provided in subsection (c), if the offense level for a career of- fender from the table in this subsection is greater than the offense level otherwise applicable, the offense level from the table in this subsection shall apply. A career offender's criminal history category in every case un- der this subsection shall be Category VI.

OFFENSE STATUTORY MAXIMUM	OFFENSE LEVEL*
(1) Life	37
(2) 25 years or more	34
(3) 20 years or more, but less than 25 years	32
(4) 15 years or more, but less than 20 years	29
(5) 10 years or more, but less than 15 years	24
(6) 5 years or more, but less than 10 years	17
(7) More than 1 year, but less than 5 years	12.

*If an adjustment from §3E1.1 (Acceptance of Responsibility) applies, de- crease the offense level by the number of levels corresponding to that ad- justment.

(c) If the defendant is convicted of 18 U.S.C. § 924(c) or § 929(a), and the de- fendant is determined to be a career offender under subsection (a), the ap- plicable guideline range shall be determined as follows:

Outside the Margin of Error

Sentencing Transcript
March 2014

55

TO DEAL WITH THIS SUBSTANCE ABUSE ISSUE. SIMPLE FACT OF THE MATTER IS YOU CANNOT CONTINUE TO SMOKE MARIJUANA DAILY OR USE ECSTASY ONCE YOU ARE RELEASED FROM PRISON. AND IT WILL GIVE YOU THE OPPORTUNITY, MR. KINZER, TO DEVELOP THE JOB SKILLS THAT YOU ARE PERFECTLY CAPABLE OF DEVELOPING SO THAT YOU CAN PURSUE A PRODUCTIVE LIFE ONCE YOU ARE RELEASED. AND I REALIZE THAT EVEN 188 MONTHS IS A LONG TIME, IT'S ABOUT 15 AND A HALF YEARS, AND THAT IS RIGHT AT THE TOP OF WHAT YOUR GUIDELINE RANGE WOULD HAVE BEEN WITHOUT CAREER OFFENDER; AND SO ARGUABLY I HAVE NOT GIVEN MUCH WEIGHT TO THE CONGRESS'S POLICY DECISION WITH RESPECT TO THE CAREER OFFENDER GUIDELINE, BUT IN THIS PARTICULAR CASE I FIND IT'S SUFFICIENT.

MR. KINZER, AS YOU KNOW, THE UNITED STATES HAS FILED A NOTICE PURSUANT TO TITLE 21, UNITED STATES CODE, SECTION 851 THAT SETS OUT YOUR PRIOR CONVICTIONS IN THIS CASE. ORDINARILY I WOULD ASK YOU TO AFFIRM OR DENY THOSE CONVICTIONS, YOU HAVE ALREADY AFFIRMED, ADMITTED THOSE CONVICTIONS IN THE PLEA AGREEMENT AND UNDER OATH HERE BEFORE THIS COURT; AND SO WE HAVE DISCUSSED PREVIOUSLY THE IMPACT OF THOSE SENTENCES ON YOUR, THOSE PRIOR SENTENCES ON YOUR RANGE OF SENTENCING HERE IN THIS COURT.

SO HAVING CONSIDERED THE NATURE AND CIRCUMSTANCES OF THE OFFENSE, OR OFFENSES, RATHER, YOUR HISTORY AND CHARACTERISTICS, THE ADVISORY GUIDELINE RANGE WHICH

56

APPLIES TO THIS CASE, AS WELL AS ALL THE OTHER FACTORS LISTED IN TITLE 18, UNITED STATES CODE, SECTION 3553(A), IT IS PURSUANT TO THE SENTENCING REFORM ACT OF 1984, THE JUDGMENT OF THE COURT THAT THE DEFENDANT, AARON KINZER, IS HEREBY COMMITTED TO THE CUSTODY OF THE BUREAU OF PRISONS TO BE IN PRISON FOR A TERM OF 188 MONTHS AS TO COUNTS 2 -- EXCUSE ME, COUNTS 1, 2 AND -- WAS IT 9?

THE CLERK: IT IS, YOUR HONOR.

THE COURT: COUNTS 1, 2 AND 9, WITH THOSE TERMS TO RUN CONCURRENTLY TO EACH OTHER, FOR A NET EFFECTIVE SENTENCE OF 188 MONTHS OF IMPRISONMENT.

I WILL RECOMMEND THAT YOU RECEIVE 500 HOURS OF SUBSTANCE ABUSE TREATMENT FROM THE BOP INSTITUTION RESIDENTIAL DRUG ABUSE TREATMENT PROGRAM. RDAP

I WILL FURTHER RECOMMEND THAT YOU BE AFFORDED A FULL RANGE OF EDUCATIONAL AND/OR VOCATIONAL PROGRAMS WHILE IN THE BUREAU OF PRISONS CUSTODY.

UPON YOUR RELEASE FROM IMPRISONMENT, YOU SHALL BE PLACED ON SUPERVISED RELEASE FOR A TERM OF 8 YEARS AS TO COUNT 1, 6 YEARS AS TO COUNT 2 AND 3 YEARS AS TO COUNT 9, WITH THOSE TERMS TO RUN CONCURRENTLY FOR A NET EFFECTIVE TERM OF 8 YEARS OF SUPERVISED RELEASE.

WITHIN 72 HOURS OF RELEASE FROM THE CUSTODY OF THE BUREAU OF PRISONS, YOU SHALL REPORT IN PERSON TO THE PROBATION OFFICE IN THE DISTRICT TO WHICH YOU HAVE BEEN

Outside the Margin of Error

Federal Prison Industries/UNICOR

Est. 1934

FCC Allenwood UNICOR - Full Time (7.00 hrs) Standard Pay Scale		Grade 5	Grade 4	Grade 3	Grade 2	Grade 1	Premium
Longevity 0 No Longevity Pay 0 to 18 Months	Hourly	$0.23	$0.46	$0.69	$0.92	$1.15	$1.35
	Daily (7.00)	$1.61	$3.22	$4.83	$6.44	$8.05	$9.45
	20 Days	$32.20	$64.40	$96.60	$128.80	$161.00	$189.00
	21 Days	$33.81	$67.62	$101.43	$135.24	$169.05	$198.45
	22 Days	$35.42	$70.84	$106.26	$141.68	$177.10	$207.90
	23 Days	$37.03	$74.06	$111.09	$148.12	$185.15	$217.35
Longevity 1 $0.10 / hour 19 to 30 Months	Hourly	$0.33	$0.56	$0.79	$1.02	$1.25	$1.45
	Daily (7.00)	$2.31	$3.92	$5.53	$7.14	$8.75	$10.15
	20 Days	$46.20	$78.40	$110.60	$142.80	$175.00	$203.00
	21 Days	$48.51	$82.32	$116.13	$149.94	$183.75	$213.15
	22 Days	$50.82	$86.24	$121.66	$157.08	$192.50	$223.30
	23 Days	$53.13	$90.16	$127.19	$164.22	$201.25	$233.45
Longevity 2 $0.15 / hour 31 to 42 Months	Hourly	$0.38	$0.61	$0.84	$1.07	$1.30	$1.50
	Daily (7.00)	$2.66	$4.27	$5.88	$7.49	$9.10	$10.50
	20 Days	$53.20	$85.40	$117.60	$149.80	$182.00	$210.00
	21 Days	$55.86	$89.67	$123.48	$157.29	$191.10	$220.50
	22 Days	$58.52	$93.94	$129.36	$164.78	$200.20	$231.00
	23 Days	$61.18	$98.21	$135.24	$172.27	$209.30	$241.50
Longevity 3 $0.20 / hour 43 to 60 Months	Hourly	$0.43	$0.66	$0.89	$1.12	$1.35	$1.55
	Daily (7.00)	$3.01	$4.62	$6.23	$7.84	$9.45	$10.85
	20 Days	$60.20	$92.40	$124.60	$156.80	$189.00	$217.00
	21 Days	$63.21	$97.02	$130.83	$164.64	$198.45	$227.85
	22 Days	$66.22	$101.64	$137.06	$172.48	$207.90	$238.70
	23 Days	$69.23	$106.26	$143.29	$180.32	$217.35	$249.55
Longevity 4 $0.25 / hour 61 to 84 Months	Hourly	$0.48	$0.71	$0.94	$1.17	$1.40	$1.60
	Daily (7.00)	$3.36	$4.97	$6.58	$8.19	$9.80	$11.20
	20 Days	$67.20	$99.40	$131.60	$163.80	$196.00	$224.00
	21 Days	$70.56	$104.37	$138.18	$171.99	$205.80	$235.20
	22 Days	$73.92	$109.34	$144.76	$180.18	$215.60	$246.40
	23 Days	$77.28	$114.31	$151.34	$188.37	$225.40	$257.60
Longevity 5 $0.30 / hour over 84 Months	Hourly	$0.53	$0.76	$0.99	$1.22	$1.45	$1.65
	Daily (7.00)	$3.71	$5.32	$6.93	$8.54	$10.15	$11.55
	20 Days	$74.20	$106.40	$138.60	$170.80	$203.00	$231.00
	21 Days	$77.91	$111.72	$145.53	$179.34	$213.15	$242.55
	22 Days	$81.62	$117.04	$152.46	$187.88	$223.30	$254.10
	23 Days	$85.33	$122.36	$159.39	$196.42	$233.45	$265.65

Hourly OT	Grade 5	Grade 4	Grade 3	Grade 2	Grade 1	Premium
Longevity 0	$0.46	$0.92	$1.38	$1.84	$2.30	$2.50
Longevity 1	$0.56	$1.02	$1.48	$1.94	$2.40	$2.60
Longevity 2	$0.61	$1.07	$1.53	$1.99	$2.45	$2.65
Longevity 3	$0.66	$1.12	$1.58	$2.04	$2.50	$2.70
Longevity 4	$0.71	$1.17	$1.63	$2.09	$2.55	$2.75
Longevity 5	$0.76	$1.22	$1.68	$2.14	$2.60	$2.80

Federal Prison Industries/UNICOR
First pay stub showing $0.23/hr

	GROSS	-	TAXES	-	POST TAX DEDUCTIONS	=	NET PAY
Curr:	14.34	-		-		=	14.34
YTD:	14.34	-		-		=	14.34

EARNINGS		RATE	HOURS	AMOUNT
8010	HOL	0.23	7.00	1.61
8020	ADM	0.23	3.00	0.69
8074	LAYIN	0.00	7.00	0.00
8510	REG	0.23	52.35	12.04

DATE COMPUTED	
HIRE DATE	02/13/2017
VACATION DATE	02/13/2017
LONGEVITY MONTHS	1.00
UNICOR WORK START	02/13/2017
ACCRUED VAC HOURS	3.50
PREV. YRS VAC HOURS	
UNPAID CALLOUT	7.00
STATUS 90	

DEDUCTIONS/ADJUSTMENT

FCC Allenwood Gathering Restriction Memo

U.S. Department of Justice Memorandum

Federal Bureau of Prisons

Federal Correctional Complex, Allenwood

Low Security Correctional Institution
P.O. Box 1500
White Deer, PA 17887

9 March 2020

MEMORANDUM FOR: INMATE POPULATION

FROM: M. Briskie, Assistant Recreation Supervisor

SUBJECT: Unauthorized Gatherings in Recreation

Gatherings of five (5) or more individuals in recreation is not authorized unless the gathering is for a Recreation sponsored event such as an intramural sports game, scheduled class, or activity. Free rec sporting events and card/board games are authorized. Gatherings for religious purposes and rap battles is prohibited. If you have any questions feel free to come by my office or see me at main line.

SUJETO: Reuniones no autorizadas en recreación

Las reuniones de cinco (5) o más personas en recreación no están autorizadas a menos que la reunión sea para un evento patrocinado por Recreación, como un juego de deportes intramuros, una clase programada o una actividad. Se autorizan eventos deportivos de recreo gratuitos y juegos de cartas/tableros. Las reuniones con fines religiosos y las batallas de rap están prohibidas. Si tiene alguna pregunta no dude en venir a mi oficina o verme en la línea principal.

FCC Allenwood Pandemic Measures Memo

MEMORANDUM FOR THE INMATE POPULATION

FROM: D.K. White, Warden

SUBJECT: BOP CORONAVIRUS (COVID-19) PROTECTIVE MEASURES

As you may be aware in talking to persons in the community, the United States is seeing an increase in the number of confirmed cases of infected persons. Effective immediately, the following actions are being taken by the Bureau of Prisons (BOP) in order to prevent or reduce the spread of COVID-19.

SCREENING OF INMATES: The BOP is screening inmates for COVID-19 using established practices:

- All newly-arriving BOP inmates are screened for COVID-19 exposure risk factors and symptoms.
- Asymptomatic inmates with exposure risk factors are being quarantined.
- Symptomatic inmates with exposure risk factors are to be isolated and tested for COVID-19 per local health authority protocols
- **To-date, no inmates have tested positive for COVID-19 in the BOP.**

SOCIAL VISITS: Social visits are suspended for 30 days, at which time the suspension will be reevaluated.

To ensure that inmates maintain community ties, inmate telephone system minutes will be increased nationally to 500 minutes per calendar month.

INMATE MOVEMENT: Inmate movement between facilities is suspended for 30 days, at which time the suspension will be reevaluated. BOP will make exceptions for special cases such as writs for prosecution on pending charges, Interstate Agreements on Detainers (IAD), medical or mental health reasons, and RRC placements. The BOP will also continue to process and admit new inmates. Other case-by-case exceptions for judicial proceedings may also be made.

Local medical trips will be made, as necessary.

LEGAL VISITS: Legal visits will be suspended for 30 days, at which time the suspension will be reevaluated. Case-by-case approval at the local level and confidential legal calls will be allowed in order to ensure access to counsel.

Access to legal counsel will be accommodated to the maximum extent practicable. *Although legal visits are generally suspended for 30-days, you may make a request to your Unit Team, who will forward it to the institution's Legal Department for review and final approval by the Warden. Attorneys will be screened prior to being admitted to the facility.*

FCC Allenwood Lockdown Memo

Information For Inmate Population

SUBJECT: LSCI Lockdown Date : April 2, 2020

On March 20, 2020, directives for a modified operation were placed in affect as a response to the global pandemic of COVID-19. As previously communicated, additional revisions would likely be implemented while combatting the spread of the virus. These directives attempt to emulate recommended public response for social distancing practices as closely as possible while countering the challenges of an open dorm setting. On April 1, 2020, updated procedures were placed in affect based on the newest and more restrictive recommendations for your health from the BOP and CDC.

The expectation of all inmates is to comply with posted directives, understand the rational supporting the modified changes, and utilize the Administrative Remedy process as the sole means to grieve alleged policy violations.

Failure to comply with staff directives jeopardizes the health and safety of all people inside the institution. The behaviors that were displayed will not be tolerated and will result in additional restrictions.

-Inmates are to remain in their assigned cubes at all times other than using the bathroom facilities.

-Inmate orderlies will be directed to clean bathrooms, fountains, and door handles hourly

-No phone or computer (email and law library) access

-All TVs to be turned off

-No commissary

-Ice rooms to be secured

-Showers will be conducted on day watch at the direction of the captain on Friday

-Sick call and pill lines to be conducted in the unit

-No work call.

-No gate pass

Poor judgement and recent incidents by the inmate population at LSCI Allenwood has led to the current Lockdown. You will remain on this status until otherwise notified. As we reduce restrictions we will return to the modified operation previously identified on April 1, 2020 to complete national quarantine for 14 days.

D.K. White, Warden

E-Mail to Warden
Complaint regarding Covid-19 housing

TRULINCS 43112074 - KINZER, AARON - Unit: ALF-U-B

FROM: 43112074
TO: LSCI Associate Wardens
SUBJECT: ***Request to Staff*** KINZER, AARON, Reg# 43112074, ALF-U-B
DATE: 08/22/2020 07:52:19 AM

To: a.w. sage/ a.w. gubiotti
Inmate Work Assignment: unicor

Why have 16 gate pass inmates been separated from the rest of Union B inmates?
If there are no positive cases as the recent memo proclaims why am I currently being quarantined inside Union B??
What is the criteria for testing inmates??
Can I be tested and once shown to be negative for covid-19 moved to another unit??

Outside the Margin of Error

Supreme Court Refusal

Case denied; Nov. 2017

Supreme Court of the United States
Office of the Clerk
Washington, DC 20543-0001

Scott S. Harris
Clerk of the Court
(202) 479-3011

November 13, 2017

Mr. Aaron Kinzer
Prisoner ID 43112-074
LSCI Butner
P.O. Box 999
Butner, NC 27509

Re: Aaron Kinzer
v. United States
No. 17-6361

Dear Mr. Kinzer:

The Court today entered the following order in the above-entitled case:

The petition for a writ of certiorari is denied.

Sincerely,

Scott S. Harris

Scott S. Harris, Clerk

Mom and Me - First Visit After 4yrs
FCI Gilmer, 2014

Bro, Mom, and Me - First Visit
FCI Gilmer, 2014

Pops and Me
USP Lee County Camp, 2018

West V Homies
FCI Gilmer 2016

Bro & Me
USP Lee County Camp, 2018

Oldest Daughter & Me
USP Lee County Camp, 2019

Youngest Kids & Me - First Visit After 7yrs
FCC Butner Low, 2017

USP Lee County Camp
2018

FCC Allenwood Low

2020

FCC Allenwood Low
Carolina Homies, 2021

S-Dot from Rochester
FCC Allenwood Low, 2021

FCC Allenwood Low
2022

FCC Allenwood Low
2022

FCC Allenwood Low
2022

Outside the Margin of Error

43112-074
KINZER
Eye: BN Ht: 6'00"
Vending
INMATE

4019 7320 0027 5577
VALID THRU 06\26
DEBIT
PERSONAL FUNDS
AARON KINZER
VISA

Bristol couple facing drug charges after search of home, business

Staff Report Oct 19, 2009 Updated Jul 1, 2020

The Sullivan County Sheriff's Office on Tuesday announced the arrests of a Bristol, Tenn., couple suspected of dealing drugs, including crack cocaine and marijuana, in the Tri-Cities.

Aaron M. Kinzer, 28, and Sandra B. Duff, 27, both of 251 Basham Hill Road, Bristol, were arrested Friday on several drug charges.

The couple's arrests followed the simultaneous execution of two search warrants about 1:45 a.m. One search warrant was for their Basham Hill Road residence and one was for Kinzer's First Class Auto business at 305 Beechwood Drive, Bristol.

BRISTOL HERALD COURIER Subscribe

JUST IN LOCALS IN COLLEGE NOTEBOOK: Bradley Bunch (...

Former Bristol, Tenn. business owner sentenced in federal drug case

GREENEVILLE, Tenn. — A man connected with one of the largest crack cocaine busts in Sullivan County was sentenced Monday in U.S. District Court for his part in a interstate drug ring.

Aaron M. Kinzer, 32, of Bristol, Tenn. will serve more than 15 years in prison after pleading guilty in July 2012 on several counts of conspiracy to distribute marijuana and crack cocaine and money laundering, the report from U.S. Attorney William Killian said.

Investigators said that Kinzer and seven other individuals would receive the drugs in either Charlotte or Atlanta and then bring them back for sale in the Tri-Cities region.

Sullivan County officers seized over $20,000 in cash and drugs, cars, boats and electronics when they raided Kinzer's home on Basham Hill Road and business on Beechwood Drive in Bristol, Tenn. in Oct. 2009.

At the business, officers located six ounces of crack cocaine estimated to be worth $15,000, another 13 individually wrapped crack rocks estimated to be worth $100 apiece. Digital scales and baggies, some with the corners cut, were also found.

Officers did not find any crack cocaine at the residence but did locate five small baggies of marijuana, a marijuana pipe with marijuana in it and two hydrocodone pills.

In addition to the drugs, SCSO vice officers seized $2,073 cash, four Oldsmobiles, a Dodge pickup, a Cobra bass boat and several electronics items. The estimated worth of items seized is believed to be between $20,000 and $25,000.

"He's a major dealer. Anybody that has six ounces of crack cocaine is a major dealer," Sheriff Wayne Anderson said of Kinzer.

Sullivan County vice officers said they'd been investigating Kinzer for about a year, and that he has a long history of drug activity involving other states as well, including Georgia and North Carolina.

For More About Aaron

Aaron M. Kinzer

Journalist. Poet. Motivational Speaker.

www.ingramcontent.com/pod-product-compliance
Lightning Source LLC
LaVergne TN
LVHW060042210926
848481LV00013B/3932
* 9 7 9 8 8 6 9 2 9 4 3 9 5 *